MADE IN AMERICA

The Annotated Donald J. Trump

Matthew O'Dell

G A R R E T T C O U N T Y P R E S S
www.gcpress.com

Garrett County Press Books are printed on acid free paper.

First Edition 2018

ISBN: 978-1-939430-19-9

DESIGNED BY COFEFE

Foreword

Matthew O'Dell exists, but O'Dell is not his name. A veteran journalist, O'Dell is someone who believes in dispassionate facts, rendered in undecorated language. If you've come to this book looking for a screed against Trump this is not for you. Anti-Trump rants are as close as the nearest phone or TV. By now even the most ardent supporters perceive that there's something a little off about Donald J. Trump. What's unique in this moment, perhaps, is the lack of a shared language to move forward. Digital networks have smashed information hierarchies and given everyone a voice, even foreign antagonists. Many supporters of the president appear to have adopted the revolutionary stance that anything can be attacked, even the recorded, videotaped, transcribed facts, if it is in service to "dismantling the administrative state."

What emerges from O'Dell's research is a work that is in accordance with generally accepted guidelines of reality. We're all tired. The internet is yelling. The TV is yelling. Friends are yelling. And they are yelling every day. Trump has taken apart our civility and turned a whole political party into a vehicle for whatever he randomly thinks at any hour of the day.

Freedom is having someone take care of the roads, bridges and schools while you do human things like love, sing, camp, rest, cook, and read. Subordination is the opposite. Subordination is having a political apparatus demand your attention every day. Trump demands it because every day he shifts the facts. He redefines truth. He threatens the most vulnerable among us.

So this book is a disciplined effort to reassert a shared truth, a shared language. It is a set of modest corrections. It isn't an argument. It is an assertion of fact from a world we once knew and will, heaven help us, know once again.

G.K. Darby,
Garrett County Press

It snowed over 4 inches this past weekend in New York City. It is still October. So much for Global Warming.[1]

3:43 PM - 1 Nov 2011

1 What Trump is describing in New York is climate (weather) — what you see out the window over a short period of time (4 inches of snow). Climate change is measured by how the atmosphere behaves over decades. Because warm air can hold more moisture, we're likely to see more powerful storms as an effect of climate change, including snow storms.

Climate change better describes — rather than global warming — the effects of increasing human-driven CO_2 levels in the atmosphere. We're already witnessing melting glaciers, increased droughts, wildfires, deluges, more powerful storms, and sea-level rise that threaten coastal, low-lying areas around the globe.

Waterboarding KSM gave us the intelligence that lead to Bin Laden.[2]

4:27 PM - 15 Nov 2011

---

2 Despite Trump's support for waterboarding, it wasn't effectively used on Khalid Sheikh Mohammed, who claimed responsibility for masterminding the 9/11 attacks and was interrogated in 2003 by the CIA in Poland.

In a 2014 report from the Senate Select Committee on Intelligence, the deputy chief of the CIA interrogation program was quoted as saying, "Against KSM it has proven ineffective. The potential for physical harm is far greater with the waterboard than with the other techniques, bringing into question the issue of risk vs. gain."

Made in America? @BarackObama called his 'birthplace' Hawaii[3]

10:54 AM - 18 Nov 2011

---

3 The false claim that Obama is secretly Muslim was first circulated by an Illinois politician in 2004, reported *Politico* in 2011.

Some Hillary Clinton supporters spread the rumor in 2008 via an anonymous chain email that was debunked by *Snopes.com* in April of that year. Trump jumped on the idea in 2011 and became the most adamant voice of the baseless claim.

Despite having no merit — and much later admitting Obama was indeed born in the U.S. — the idea was picked up and spread by half a dozen Fox News hosts and analysts.

Newly released emails prove that scientists have manipulated data on global warming. The data is unreliable.[4]

1:25 PM - 30 Nov 2011

4 The *WSJ* article Trump is citing here is written by known climate denier and Brietbart editor, James Delingpole, who admits that he is not a scientist and has no science background.

According to a 2016 study in the journal *Environmental Research Letters*, "The consensus that humans are causing recent global warming is shared by 90%–100% of publishing climate scientists. Those results are consistent with the 97% consensus reported by Cook et al (Environ. Res. Lett. 8 024024) based on 11,944 abstracts of research papers."

I feel sorry for Rosie's new partner in love whose parents are devastated at the thought of their daughter being with @Rosie –a true loser.[5]

11:45 AM - 14 Dec 2011

---

[5] It can be puzzling to understand why Trump feuds with various celebrities, but this one seems to have started in 2006, when O'Donnell skewered him on *The View* after he publicly forgave a Miss USA winner (a pageant where he had an ownership stake) for "drinking, using drugs and ... kissing a woman," reported the *New York Times*. She mocked him and pointed out the hypocrisy of the double divorcee, whose previous marriages ended amid alleged infidelity.

The slight appeared to fuel a grudge, with tweets from Trump over the years – and criticism from O'Donnell – as well as mentions about the comedian on the campaign trail and even the first presidential debate.

Barney Frank looked disgusting–nipples protruding–in his blue shirt before Congress. Very very disrespectful.[6]

3:36 PM - 21 Dec 2011

---

6 Stirring controversy online isn't unique to Trump, but he's certainly mastered the form. In an interview on *Fox News with Tucker Carlson*, Trump said: "I think that maybe I wouldn't be here if it wasn't for Twitter, because I get such a fake press, such a dishonest press."

A study says @Autism is out of control–a 78% increase in 10 years. Stop giving monstrous combined vaccinations immediately. Space out small individual shots–small babies can't handle massive doses. Get smart–and fast–before it is too late.[7]

10:25 AM - 30 Mar 2012

---

7 The American Academy of Pediatrics has released several statements rebuking tweets like this.

In 2012: "Science has shown there is a clear genetic component to ASD [autism spectrum disorder]. Scientists are also studying many of the changes in our environment over the past two decades that may interact with genes to increase a person's risk of developing symptoms of autism. Large epidemiologic studies, such as the National Children's Study, funded by the National Institutes of Health, will be able to track what children are exposed to and their likelihood of developing autism, which will give some valuable clues.

"One exposure that has been extensively studied is vaccines. The AAP wants to reassure parents that all signs show no link between vaccines and autism. Many studies have looked at this, and none has found a link. Parents who have questions about vaccines are encouraged to talk with their child's pediatrician, who can provide scientifically validated information about immunizations."

In 2015, the AAP issued this response to Republican primary debate remarks: "Claims that vaccines are linked to autism, or are unsafe when administered according to the recommended schedule, have been disproven by a robust body of medical literature. It is dangerous to public health to suggest otherwise."

He @BarackObama wants 23 years of @MittRomney's tax returns. Let's see BHO's school applications, transcripts and Rezkko deals. I wonder what they say about his place of birth–how were his grades (I think I know). Demand their release.[8]

3:29 PM - 10 Apr 2012

---

8 Earl Ofari Hutchinson wrote in *Los Angeles Daily News*, "Obama has effectively put his birth certificate issue to rest with the release of his official long-form certificate. His alleged academic failings will become another distraction. The point of this foolish issue is not just to take another cheap shot at Obama, but to use it as a ploy to question Obama's wisdom and capability on the fiscal, economic and foreign policy positions that Tea Party leaders and activists, and much of the GOP relentlessly oppose."

According to @BarackObama the War on Terror is over but global warming is a national security threat. Feel safe?[9]

4:12 PM - 4 May 2012

---

9 Pentagon officials said in a 2015 report, "Climate change is a security risk because it degrades living conditions, human security and the ability of governments to meet the basic needs of their populations. Communities and states that already are fragile and have limited resources are significantly more vulnerable to disruption and far less likely to respond effectively and be resilient to new challenges. To reduce the national security implications of climate change, combatant commands are integrating climate-related impacts into their planning cycles."

I want to see @ BarackObama's college records to see how he listed his place of birth in the application.

12:44 PM - 30 May 2012

Isn't it ironic that President Obama, of all people, is pushing for 'universal background checks?!'[10]

4:22 PM - 27 Feb 2013

---

10 On *The Tonight Show* in 2012, President Obama joked that Trump's anger toward him was part of a long-running feud.

I am impressed with the scam @BarackObama pulled, but the truth will come out.

9:29 AM - 20 Jul 2012

Obama joked: "This all dates back to when we were growing up together in Kenya ..."

In his own words, @BarackObama "was born in Kenya, and raised in Indonesia and Hawaii." This statement was made, in writing, in the 1990's. Why does the press protect him? Is this another Watergate?

2:13 PM - 30 May 2012

"... We had, you know, constant run-ins on the soccer field. He wasn't very good, resented it ..."

What a coincidence– Michelle Obama called Kenya @BarackObama's "homeland" in 2008

10:02 AM - 29 Aug 2012

"... When we finally moved to America, I thought it would be over."

When will we see @BarackObama's passport records (sealed)?[11]

4:18 PM - 17 Jul 2012

---

11 Trump's flirtation with conspiracy theories is well known and wide-ranging. In 2012, he posted a web video offering $5 million to charity if Obama would make public his college transcripts and passport.

Weird–why did BarackObama Sr. fail to list @BarackObama as his son in his 1961 INS application?[12]

10:26 AM - 18 Jul 2012

---

12 Trump passed this a long from a far-right web site called *WorldNetDaily*, which took donations in order to post billboards that said, "Where's the birth certificate?"

A reporter from the publication named Lester Kinsolving attended a White House Press conference, which went like this (via *Politifact*):

White House spokesman Robert Gibbs: "Are you looking for the president's birth certificate?"

Kinsolving: "Yes."

Gibbs: "It's on the Internet, Lester."

Kinsolving: "No, no, no – the long form listing his hospital and physician."

Gibbs: "Lester ... This question in many ways continues to astound me. The state of Hawaii provided a copy, with a seal, of the president's birth. I know there are apparently at least 400,000 people that continue to doubt the existence of and the certification by the state of Hawaii of the president's birth there, but it's on the Internet because we put it on the Internet for each of those 400,000 to download."

Congratulations to @RealSheriffJoe on his successful Cold Case Posse investigation which claims @BarackObama's 'birth certificate' is fake[13]

11:56 AM - 18 Jul 2012

13 Former Maricopa County (Arizona) Sheriff Joe Arpaio's "Cold Case Posse" conducted an investigation into Obama's birth certificate for five years, even after the birth certificate had been posted online by the White House and the story was proved to be false. Arpaio's predecessor disbanded the effort.

On Aug. 25, 2017, President Trump pardoned the former sheriff of a criminal contempt conviction. The misdemeanor conviction came after Arpaio defied a judge who ordered him to stop detaining immigrants who lacked legal status.

At least 12 dead and 50 wounded in Colorado–bring back fast trials & death penalty for mass murderers & terrorists.[14]

9:19 AM - 20 Jul 2012

---

14 The tweet refers to the Aurora, Colorado, mass shooting in 2012 at a movie theater showing a Batman sequel, *The Dark Knight Rises*. James E. Holmes was convicted of the murders in 2015.

Trump appears to make a distinction between murders and terrorists here. Holmes, like most white mass shooters, was never treated as a terrorist.

With @BarackObama listing himself as "Born in Kenya" in HI laws allowed him to produce a fake certifi-cate. #SCAM[15]

10:07 AM - 20 Jul 2012

---

15 Via *Politifact*:

After "numerous requests" for Obama's birth certificate, the director of the Hawaii Department of Health, Dr. Chiyome Fukino, put out this statement: "State law prohibits the release of a certified birth certificate to persons who do not have a tangible interest in the vital record."

"Therefore I, as director of health for the state of Hawaii, along with the registrar of Vital Statistics who has statutory authority to oversee and maintain these type of vital records, have personally seen and verified that the Hawaii State Department of Health has Sen. Obama's original birth certificate on record in accordance with state policies and procedures."

An 'extremely credible source' has called my office & told me that @BarackObama applied to Occidental as a foreign student—think about it![16]

4:20 PM - 6 Aug 2012

---

16 It appears that Trump's claim was largely circulating amid birther social media. These sources have gone to extremes, such as creating fake documents, including a false Columbia student ID.

Massive combined inoculations to small children is the cause for big increase in autism.....

3:22 PM - 23 Aug 2012

Look what happened to the autism rate from 1983-2008 since one-time massive shots were given to children.[17]

4:59 PM - 27 Aug 2012

---

17 Trump seems to have been influenced by a discredited former British doctor named Andrew Wakefield, who was charged by the U.K. General Medical Council with fraud.

No more massive injections. Tiny children are not horses —one vaccine at a time, over time.

9:29 AM - 3 Sep 2014

Wakefield attended Trump's inauguration ball, according to *The Times of London*, and provided Trump with a documentary called *Vaxxed*.

So many people who have children with autism have thanked me—amazing response. They know far better than fudged up reports!

4:20 PM - 6 Aug 2012

Wakefield claimed CDC scientists had, through a government conspiracy, committed crimes worse than "Stalin, Pol Pot and Hitler."

Wake Up America! See article: "Israeli Science: Obama Birth Certificate is a Fake"[18]

11:40 AM - 13 Sep 2012

18 Despite years of claiming to the contrary, as in this tweet, Trump reversed his position in September 2016, stating, "President Barack Obama was born in the United States, period." He made the announcement at his Washington, D.C. hotel, after calling the media there to report on veterans' endorsements of his campaign, and to praise his new venue ("I think it may be one of the great hotels anywhere in the world," he said). "Now we all want to get back to making America strong and great again."

Obama's '07 speech which @DailyCaller just released not only shows that Obama is a racist but also how the press always covers for him.[19]

3:44 PM - 3 Oct 2012

---

19 Trump, who was sued in the 1970s, because he would not rent apartments in one building in New York City to African American tenants, often calls people racist without explaining why. Frequently the people accused of racism are African Americans, including Bryant Gumbel, the writer and cultural critic Touré, and PBS talk show host Tavis Smiley. He's also called the name of the TV show *Blackish* racist.

Got to do something about these missing chidlren grabbed by the perverts. Too many incidents–fast trial, death penalty.[20]

9:13 AM - 8 Oct 2012

---

20 Long before popular talk of "fake news," Trump was still propagating a false narrative begun in the 1980s – that thousands of children were abducted by strangers. The storyline was helped along by photos of missing children on milk cartons, which, as Stephen Buckley wrote in the *Tampa Bay Times*, ignored more likely causes for the children to be missing: "custody battle, or some other dispute, gone dreadfully wrong. The random kidnappings weren't random at all. We still see the impact of that false narrative in the don't-ride-your-bicycle-more-than-a-block-from-the-house paranoia that possesses parents today."

This tweet also raises the question: What is the point of a trial if it unfailingly leads to the death penalty? And if that's the case, why does it matter if a kangaroo court is sufficiently speedy?

RT @ReutersPolitics: Trump to give $5 million to charity if Obama releases records[21]

3:59 PM - 11 Oct 2012

21 In October, shortly before the 2012 presidential election, Trump went on *The Late Show with David Letterman* and said he'd give $5 million to the charity of Obama's choice if he'd release his college and passport records.

Attention all hackers: You are hacking everything else so please hack Obama's college records (destroyed?) and check "place of birth"[22]

6:06 AM - 6 Sep 2014

---

22 "For five years, he has led the birther movement to delegitimize our first black president," Hillary Clinton said after Trump gave up the birther conspiracies in September 2016. "His campaign was founded on this outrageous lie."

Autism rates through the roof–why doesn't the Obama administration do something about doctor-inflicted autism. We lose nothing to try.[23]

12:19 PM - 22 Oct 2012

---

23 According to a March 2016 CDC report "an estimated 1 in 68 (14.6 per 1,000) school-aged children have been identified with autism spectrum disorder (ASD). This report shows essentially no change in ASD prevalence, the proportion of school aged-children with ASD, from the previous report released in 2014."

Sarah Jessica Parker voted "unsexiest woman alive" – I agree. She said "it's beneath me to comment on the potential Obama charitable gift." What's really beneath her?[24]

4:05 PM - 26 Oct 2012

---

24 Trump's body shaming has targeted celebrities including Angelina Jolie, Halle Berry, and at least one Kardashian.

Parker in March 2017 trolled Trump with a photo that showed her *Sex and the City* character Carrie Bradshaw in an Instagram post wondering if she had been the only one who hadn't been invited to meet with Russian ambassador Sergey Kislyak.

The Russian foreign ministry on its Twitter account weighed in:

"If #SarahJessicaParker desperately wants to meet Russian Ambassador to US -anything is possible. Sergey Ivanovich will be happy."

While @BetteMidler is an extremely unattractive woman, I refuse to say that because I always insist on being politically correct.[25]

11:59 AM - 28 Oct 2012

---

25 This may be in response to one of Bette Middler's tweets, two days earlier in 2012, in which she wrote: "Donald Trump architect of the ruination of the West Side, deserves to be held down and his hair cut off, or strapped to the roof of the car!"

The President has until tomorrow at 12 noon to pick up $5M for his favorite charity. Looking like he won't be doing it. What is he hiding?[26]

10:30 AM - 31 Oct 2012

26 After Trump admitted in 2016 that Obama was born in the United States, *The Washington Post's* David Fahrenthold wrote "a $5 million gift from Trump's own pocket now would be more than the GOP nominee has given to charity in the last 20 years, combined."

Global warming is based on faulty science and manipulated data which is proven by the emails that were leaked[27]

2:59 PM - 2 Nov 2012

27 According to Charles Miller, a research scientist at NASA's Jet Propulsion Laboratory, "Current CO2 values are more than 100 [parts per million] higher than at any time in the last one million years — and maybe higher than any time in the last 25 million years. These increases in atmospheric CO2 are causing real, significant changes in the Earth system now, not in some distant future climate, and will continue to be felt for centuries to come. We can study these impacts to better understand the way the Earth will respond to future changes, but unless serious actions are taken immediately, we risk the next threshold being a point of no return in mankind's unintended global-scale geoengineering experiment."

The concept of global warming was created by and for the Chinese in order to make U.S. manufacturing non-competitive.[28]

2:15 PM - 6 Nov 2012

---

28 Trump's talk on climate change resembles other statements that free the way for industrial deregulation related to environmental policy.

During a presidential debate with Hillary Clinton on Sept 26, 2015 in New York, Clinton said that Trump "thinks that climate change is a hoax perpetrated by the Chinese." Trump responded: "I did not – I did not – I do not say that. I do not say that."

"I think the climate change is just a very, very expensive form of tax," Trump said of Fox News on January 18, 2016. This interview presents a strange contradiction, where Trump seems to suggest that China is destroying the environment, and, at the same time, the country is undercutting U.S. business because of lack of regulation. It's not entirely clear where he stands.

Sorry losers and haters, but my I.Q. is one of the highest – and you all know it! Please don't feel so stupid or insecure, it's not your fault[29]

6:37 PM - 8 May 2013

29 Trump's family history, often incorrectly described as Swedish, is in fact, traced back to a German village, which *The Economist* described in 2016: "The people of Kallstadt are affectionately known as Brulljesmacher, meaning braggart in the regional dialect."

How come every time I show anger, disgust or impatience, enemies say I had a tantrum or meltdown—stupid or dishonest people?[30]

3:21 PM - 12 Nov 2012

---

30 This tweet was picked up and published in an article about celebrities and social media titled "Dumb and dumberer," in the *Toronto Sun*. It is quintessential Trump hitting back.

It makes me feel so good to hit "sleazebags" back – much better than seeing a psychiatrist (which I never have!)[31]

11:06 AM - 19 Nov 2012

---

31 Sleazebag is a favorite Trump insult and has been hurled at reporters asking about claims of sexual assault and Timothy L. O'Brien, who Trump sued over his book *Trump Nation: The Art of Being the Donald.*

It's amazing that people can say such bad things about me but if I say bad things about them, it becomes a national incident.[32]

3:24 PM - 9 Jan 2013

32 Trump often uses the word "bad" twice in tweets, yet another unusual linguistic tick. See next tweets…

Everybody is arguing whether or not it is a BAN. Call it what you want, it is about keeping bad people (with bad intentions) out of country!

7:50 AM - 1 Feb 2017

If the ban were announced with a one week notice, the "bad" would rush into our country during that week. A lot of bad "dudes" out there!

8:31 AM - 30 Jan 2017

I'm really saddened to see that @ Cher was voted "the 4th ugliest celebrity" according to @listverse....[33]

7:50 AM - 1 Feb 2017

---

33 In 2011, Cher tweeted that she would see Trump around Aspen and that he was a "major ass."

On his February 1, 2017 show, Howard Stern said of Trump, "He wants to be liked, he wants to be loved. He loves Hollywood. First of all, he loves the press. He lives for it. He loves people in Hollywood. He only wants to hobnob with them. All of this hatred and stuff directed towards him. There's a reason every president who leaves the office has grey hair."

@michelle-malkin You were born stupid![34]

10:10 AM - 22 Mar 2013

34 The conservative blogger Michelle Malkin raised Trump's ire starting in 2011 after calling him a conservative fraud and criticizing him for trying to use eminent domain to secure private property for private development.

Looks like the U.S. will be having the coldest March since 1996-global warming any-one???????[35]

4:07 PM - 22 Mar 2013

---

35 According to NOAA and NASA, four of the five hottest years on record have occurred since 2013. The five hottest years since 1850, when temperature records began, have all occurred since 2010.

@michellemalkin & @BuzzFeedAndrew: "Vaccine court awards millions to two autistic children damaged by vaccine"[36]

4:07 PM - 22 Mar 2013

---

36 *The Natural News* website that Trump refers to cites a story in the *Huffington Post*. That article states that the children were compensated for vaccine-induced encephalopathy, which caused permanent damage. The families claim the brain damage has resulted in autism. Neither the court nor the U.S. Department of Health and Human Services has ever conceded that the two children in question have autism.

From the U.S. Department of HHS: "According to the CDC, from 2006 to 2015 over 2.8 billion doses of covered vaccines were distributed in the U.S. For petitions filed in this time period, 4,426 petitions were adjudicated by the Court, and of those 2,884 were compensated. This means for every 1 million doses of vaccine that were distributed, 1 individual was compensated."

@realBrianBuxton: @fluffyguy why is @realDonaldTrump even at a @wwe event?" Ratings asshole - I'll bet in life you are a very big failure!³⁷

7:22 AM - 7 Apr 2013

---

37 Brendan Brown, who runs the excellent *Trump Twitter Archive*, told *The Washington Post* that Trump's tweets all land in one of three categories: praise/compliments, insults he's responding to, and news/opinions that put him in a favorable light and/or others in an unfavorable light. When Trump is responding, there is often a certain disproportion in the vitriol of the response compared to the perceived insult of the original tweet.

Via @financial-post: "Climate changing for global warming journalists" by Lawrence Solomon http://bit.ly/ZxJNyk Consensus is "cracking."[38]

3:45 PM - 16 Apr 2013

---

38 The eight warmest years on record, according to NOAA, are: 2016, 2015, 2014, 2010, 2013, 2005, 2009, and 1998. And there hasn't been a record-cold year since 1911. Because of the warm tropical Pacific Ocean trend called El Niño that occurred in 2016, 2017 is not likely to be warmer than 2016, but is likely to still be one of the hottest on record, says the U.K. Met Office.

Should be public execution for all to see – you will end this bullshit fast![39]

8:05 PM - 19 Apr 2013

---

39 Convicted Boston Marathon bomber Dzhokhar Tsarnaev was sentenced to death in 2015 for the 2013 bombing at the Boston Marathon.

With Boston terrorist cell widening in suspects, it's now clear that it was a mistake to read the bomber the Miranda warning so early.

12:37 PM - 2 May 2013

In 2013, when the then-suspect was arrested, authorities actually delayed reading him his rights, citing what's called the public-safety exception, which would have allowed any statements he made be admissible as evidence even before his Miranda rights had been read.

@scottygam: @realDonaldTrump Jon Stewart calls you F**ckface Von Clownstick. What's that all about?" He's an overrated asshole – total phoney.[40]

9:43 PM - 2 May 2013

40 In *Politifact*, Linda Qiu wrote, "Just before he jumped into the presidential race, Trump reignited his spat with Jon Stewart, calling the comedian 'a wiseguy with no talent' and denying that he ever attacked Stewart for not using his real last name, Leibowitz. But Trump did go after Stewart's use of a stage name in a series of tweets that many took to be anti-Semitic."

@dlayphoto: @realDonaldTrump Is that why you've filed for bankruptcy numerous times?" I never filed for bankruptcy asshole![41]

10:18 PM - 8 May 2013

---

41 "Attitudes are more important than facts," wrote Dr. Norman Vincent Peale in *The Power of Positive Thinking*. "Any fact facing us, however difficult, even seemingly hopeless, is not so important as our attitude toward that fact. A confident and optimistic thought pattern can modify or overcome the fact altogether."

Peale, a celebrity pastor and author, ministered to Trump and his family at Marble Collegiate Church in Manhattan.

Trump has admitted he filed for bankruptcy four times: in 1991, 1992, 2004, and 2009, according to a fact check by *The Tampa Bay Times* in 2015.

For all of the morons who have been complaining about my comment on sexual assault & rape in the military, don't you see that it was asked as a question, with a question mark at the end of the sentence! In other words, it wasn't made as a statement, but rather as a question. I wanted your views. Many of the generals and military officials were not in favor of the male/female mix. What do you think of that?![42]

12:08 PM - 9 May 2013

---

42 On May 7, 2013, Trump tweeted: "26,000 unreported sexual assults in the military-only 238 convictions. What did these geniuses expect when they put men & women together?"

The *Los Angeles Times* reported in 2014, according to the Pentagon, an estimated "19,000 troops were victims of 'unwanted sexual contact' – down from an estimated 26,000 two years earlier."

"@danrpriest: @realDonaldTrump Just out of curiosity, what makes you care so much about what they think?" I study cowards and stupid people[43]

5:25 PM - 24 May 2013

---

43 "Stupid people" is another vague Trump insult, like "losers" and "haters" used when retaliating via Twitter.

It's freezing outside, where the hell is "global warming"??[44]

7:00 PM - 25 May 2013

---

44 This appears to be a fundamental misunderstanding or deliberate faux-misunderstanding of the term global warming.

A 2015 report from the Alliance for a Greater New York (ALIGN), a coalition of labor and environmental activists, found that Trump's buildings are some of the worst contributors to climate change in New York. While a reported energy use retrofit of the Empire State Building cut energy use by almost 40 percent, Trump Tower, the report said, uses more energy than 93 percent of large residential buildings in the city.

"@CoolChange80: @realDonaldTrump Are you really calling for the execution of #Snowden ." He is a traitor, absolutely. Others won't follow! [45]

9:15 PM - 25 Jun 2013

45 Trump's pro-execution stance goes at least as far back as his full-page ad in 1989 in the *New York Daily News* calling for the execution of five black and Latino teens in the Central Park jogger case, who were later exonerated.

"@sonaderi: @realDonaldTrump @coolchange80 And you're okay with the government spying on you?" Must have power to stop terrorists etc.[46]

9:26 PM - 25 Jun 2013

---

46 Despite tough talk on surveillance, Trump seems particularly not OK with the government spying on him, and took criticism for a series of tweets in 2017 that claimed the Obama administration had wiretapped Trump Tower without offering any evidence.

Call it any way you like, but Snowden is a traitor. When our country was great do you know what we did to traitors?[47]

3:41 PM - 27 Jun 2013

47 Trump frequently uses repetition where others might vary their words. "Nearly every example of his rhetoric that I've looked at has this repetitive cadence, to a degree that is strikingly different from other politicians of this era," wrote University of Pennsylvania linguist Mark Liberman in his blog.

"@EDM____HEAD: @realDonaldTrump @EdandBev lyin ass nigga" Why does Paula D get destroyed and you can use the "N" word so freely, asshole??[48]

8:31 PM - 30 Jun 2013

48 According to a report in the *Chicago Tribune* on August 14, 2017: "Trump has directed accusations of racism toward black people three times as often as he's done so against whites." That same report noted three of the seven white people Trump has accused of racism are David Letterman, Hillary Clinton, and Elizabeth Warren.

Isn't it crazy that people of little or no talent or success can be so critical of those whose accomplishments are great with no retribution[49]

8:19 AM - 18 Jul 2013

---

49 In the magazine he led for 25 years, *Vanity Fair*, Graydon Carter wrote, "Just to drive him a little bit crazy, I took to referring to him as a 'short-fingered vulgarian' in the pages of *Spy* magazine. To this day, I receive the occasional envelope from Trump. Like the other packages, this one included a circled hand and the words ... written in gold Sharpie: 'See, not so short!' I sent the picture back by return mail with a note attached, saying, 'Actually, quite short.' Which I can only assume gave him fits."

"@fam5rock: @realDonaldTrump #snowden not a traitor. Shared info with fellow Americans who have a right to know about NSA snooping" Bullshit[50]

4:35 PM - 27 Jul 2013

---

50 Despite Trump attacking Snowden for hacked information, Trump had no problem using the DNC hacked messages to his advantage, without condemning the hacking.

He also openly called for Russia to hack Clinton.

After the DNC phishing attack of Clinton's emails – which the director of National Intelligence and the Department of Homeland Security attributed to the Russian government – Trump took to the campaign trail saying the hacked messages showed "how much is at stake in November and how unattractive and dishonest our country has become."

@lefthandedrant: @realDonaldTrump @HuffingtonPost@ ariannahuff they re-run stories every hour....and yes she is as goofy as she is dopey[51]

9:50 PM - 12 Aug 2013

51 Referring to the *Huffington Post*, Trump told *The New York Observer* in 2012: "The trash they write about me is not reporting, there are so many inaccuracies about me on her site. "I won't hold back when I respond about her to my 1.4 million Twitter followers." Trump claimed to have raised the rent on an apartment at his building at 502 Park Avenue to $100,000 a month to keep Arianna Huffington from renting it after the AOL buyout of her blog.

You must admit that Bryant Gumbel is one of the dumbest racists around – an arrogant dope with no talent. Failed at CBS etc – why still on TV?[52]

11:21 PM - 20 Aug 2013

---

52 The Gumbel-hosted HBO show *Real Sports* covered Trump's plan to create a luxury golf course, hotel and housing along untouched dunes and North Sea coast in Scotland. The plan caused protests from locals.

"Gumbel goes on HBO to cover the amazing story of a golf course I am building in Scotland," Trump wrote in the 2011 book *Time To Get Tough: Make America Great Again!* "…and goes off on a rant about me and Obama and tries to paint me as some kind of racist."

Why are people upset w/ me over Pres Obama's birth certificate?I got him to release it, or whatever it was, when nobody else could![53]

4:41 PM - 22 Aug 2013

---

53 *New Republic* contributing editor John McWhorter wrote on NPR.org, "Trump's style of speaking clearly reflects an unusual degree of narcissism. The pride he repeatedly mentioned was for forcing the release of the birth certificate — when the release was in fact a repudiation of his claims that such a document did not exist."

@MrMarin88: Why does @realDonaldTrump always insist on calling ppl names and trying to taunt like a kid in a schoolyard? Only stupid people[54]

10:04 PM - 9 Sep 2013

54 Many Trump tweets are a reaction to criticism, but this one really stands out, elegantly, spectacularly confirming the critique itself.

President Obama wants to change the name of the "White House" because it is highly discriminating and not at all politically correct[55]

9:19 AM - 8 Oct 2013

---

55 This is an example of a race-baiting, dog-whistle strategy that appears to address political correctness but actually sends a message to a group that wanted to delegitimize Obama's presidency.

ObamaCare is a disaster and Snowden is a spy who should be executed-but if it and he could reveal Obama's records, I might become a major fan[56]

6:48 PM - 30 Oct 2013

---

56 Trump repeatedly called Snowden a traitor – and called for his execution – but here reverses course as he returns to birtherism.

Denver, Minnesota and others are bracing for some of the coldest weather on record. What are the global warming geniuses saying about this?[57]

6:42 PM - 3 Dec 2013

---

57 In 2014, the World Meteorological Organization reported that 2013 was, at the time, the sixth hottest year on record. The ranking was based on data from NASA, NOAA and the UK Met Office, according to Climate Central.

Ice storm rolls from Texas to Tennessee - I'm in Los Angeles and it's freezing. Global warming is a total, and very expensive, hoax![58]

10:13 AM - 6 Dec 2013

---

58 Trump – and to be fair he's far from being alone – appears to be unaware or ignores the difference between short-term weather and decades-long global temperature averages.

It is really too bad that the scientists studying **GLOBAL WARMING** in Antarctica got stuck on their icebreaker because of massive ice and cold[59]

7:02 AM - 27 Dec 2013

---

59 The BBC reported that the expedition, made up of researchers and tourists, was doomed by bad logistics and a questionable call to move ahead despite a bad weather forecast. Again, weather vs. climate change.

@Michael_KSC: @realDonaldTrump @thedropkicks Whether Global Warming or Climate change. The fact is We didn't cause it. We cannot change it.[60]

6:42 AM - 18 Feb 2014

60 This tweet marks an interesting shift in rhetoric. Instead of denying climate change or calling it a hoax, Trump seems to suggest it's occurring but is not caused by humans.

A frequently cited stat is that 97% of scientists agree global warming is human driven. That's not quite correct. The figure reflects the opinion of scientists who have studied climate change, and indeed 97% of them agree humans burning fossil fuels cause the problem.

If I were President I would push for proper vaccinations but would not allow one time massive shots that a small child cannot take – AUTISM.[61]

7:44 PM - 27 Mar 2014

61 Trump's own pick for Health Secretary, Rep. Tom Price (R-Ga.), when asked during his confirmation hearing if vaccines cause autism said: "The science on that is that it does not." Price was later forced to resign after reports of his government-funded use of private jets.

Snowden is a spy who has caused great damage to the U.S. A spy in the old days, when our country was respected and strong, would be executed[62]

8:29 PM - 18 Apr 2014

---

62 Trump again goes straight to a call for execution in this tweet, favoring authoritarian-style justice instead of due process.

With our border not being secure, Obama is giving a pathway to terrorists to enter our country. An attack is on him.[63]

4:42 PM - 17 Jun 2014

---

63 There has been no terrorist attack committed on U.S. soil related to the southern U.S. border.

The American people are sick and tired of not being able to lead normal lives and to constantly be on the lookout for terror and terrorists!

4:44 PM - 22 May 2016

As president, Trump's second attempt at a travel ban of predominantly Muslim countries (the first was struck down by a judge in Seattle) was halted by federal judges in Hawaii and Maryland.

"It is a lesson that presidents usually learn quickly," wrote Michael D. Shear in *The New York Times*. "Difficult and controversial issues can easily be painted as black-and-white during a long campaign, but they are often more complicated for those who are in a position to govern."

The Central Park Five documentary was a one sided piece of garbage that didn't explain the.horrific crimes of these young men while in park[64]

3:34 AM - 24 Apr 2013

---

64 In 1989, Trump called for the death penalty to be reinstated in New York, after five teenagers from Harlem were accused of beating and raping a white female jogger in Central Park. Four of the five teens, after hours of interrogation, signed wildly different accounts and admitted being at the scene of the crime. But their sentences were overturned after DNA evidence and the detailed confession pointed to the guilt of a serial rapist.

I'd bet the lawyers for the Central Park 5 are laughing at the stupidity of N.Y.C. when there was such a strong case against their "clients"

7:23 AM - 22 Jun 2014

Trump maintained as late as 2014 that the teenagers were guilty despite evidence that overturned their convictions. "These young men do not exactly have the pasts of angels," Trump wrote in a *New York Daily News* op-ed. None of the teens had been previously convicted of a crime.

Must read @ny-post editorial on $40M NYC tax-payer settlement to Central Park Thugs –

4:44 PM - 22 May 2016

Sarah Burns, who co-directed the documentary *The Central Park Five*, wrote in a 2016 *New York Times* op-ed, "The idea that teenagers who were in a park while crimes were being committed by others deserved to be labeled rapists and sent to prison for between 8 and 13 years is an affront to our Constitution."

The animal who beheaded the woman in Oklahoma should be given a very fast trial and then the death penalty. The same fate – beheading?[65]

10:10 PM - 26 Sep 2014

---

65 A man did in fact behead a woman – and stab another female employee – after being fired at a Vaughan Foods store in Moore, Oklahoma. After the ghastly act, a photo was taken of police briefing store employees about the situation. What may have caught Trump's attention was that the photo was circulated under the tag line: "Wow! Muslims shouting 'Praise Allah' surround Oklahoma cops after a press conference on the beheading in Oklahoma."

According to Snopes.com, "there were no Muslims present who were shouting 'Praise Allah!' or reading from the Quran. Moore Police Department Public Affairs Officer Jeremy Lewis was asked if there was a group of Muslims protesting the scene, and he stated, 'No, there was not.'"

Trump has tweeted the phrase "fast (or quick) trial" followed by "death penalty," half a dozen times and generally called for the death penalty for various cases at least twice as many times.

Every time I speak of the haters and losers I do so with great love and affection. They cannot help the fact that they were born fucked up![66]

8:21 PM - 28 Sep 2014

---

66 Trump, whose father encouraged his sons to be "killers," later in an unrelated tweet wrote: "When someone attacks me, I always attack back ... except 100x more. This has nothing to do with a tirade but rather, a way of life!"

Virgin Group owner Richard Branson, in a blog post, detailed a lunch with Trump that illustrates his penchant for revenge.

"Even before the starters arrived he began telling me about how he had asked a number of people for help after his latest bankruptcy and how five of them were unwilling to help," Branson wrote. "He told me he was going to spend the rest of his life destroying these five people. He didn't speak about anything else and I found it very bizarre."

What the hell is Obama doing in allowing all of these potentially very sick people to continue entering the U.S.! Is he stupid or arrogant?[67]

6:13 PM - 5 Oct 2014

---

67 Trump wasn't the only one who called for a travel ban from West African nations affected by the 2014 Ebola outbreak. *The Atlantic* reported at the time that some Senate Democrats – especially those who sought reelection in 2016 – supported a ban while others called for travel restrictions for those who may have been exposed to Ebola.

Then-CDC Director Tom Frieden wrote in a blog post that a ban would "increase the risk that Ebola will spread in those countries and to other countries, and that we will have more patients who develop Ebola in the U.S."

Two Americans eventually contracted Ebola in the United States and were treated successfully. By November 10, 2014, the last U.S. Ebola patient had been cured.

Obama is looking like an incompetent fool in the handling of the war against. ISIS! Why isn't China and Russia helping - they gain so much![68]

8:20 AM - 8 Oct 2014

---

68 Trump attacked Obama for creating a vacuum for ISIS by withdrawing U.S. troops. In 2007, Trump told CNN that Iraq was "a total catastrophe and you might as well get out now, because you just are wasting time."

Ratings challenged @CNN reports so seriously that I call President Obama (and Clinton) "the founder" of ISIS, & MVP. THEY DON'T GET SARCASM?- Donald J. Trump (@realDonaldTrump)[69]

8:20 AM - 8 Oct 2014

---

69 Trump here claims that his previous remarks were meant sarcastically, which suggests a fundamental misunderstanding on his part on why people found these comments troubling, as well as those that Obama is Muslim and was born outside the U.S.

Just out - the POLAR ICE CAPS are at an all time high, the POLAR BEAR population has never been stronger. Where the hell is global warming?[70]

5:15 AM - 29 Oct 2014

70 The International Union for Conservation of Nature currently classifies polar bears as "vulnerable" – at high risk of extinction in the wild.

However, some polar bear populations across the world have stabilized or increased. In 2014, the IUCN reported that of the 19 subpopulations of wild polar bears, one subpopulation had actually grown, six were stable and three were in decline. There wasn't enough data to make a call on the other nine populations.

However, that doesn't mean that polar ice is growing as Trump suggests, or that climate change isn't a problem or that climate change isn't a threat to the polar bear population.

Polar bears need sea ice to hunt, and some climate scientists estimate the Arctic will see ice-free summers by the 2030s.

A December 2016, study in the Royal Society's *Biology Letters*, estimates a 70 percent chance that the current population – 26,000 – will drop by more than 30 percent over the next 35 years.

Sadly, because president Obama has done such a poor job as president, you won't see another black president for generations! [71]

3:15 AM - 25 Nov 2014

71 Obama's approval rating at the time of this tweet was at an all-time low, 40 percent, according to Gallup.

NBC News reported "pollsters attribute the wide discontent to the lingering effects of the Great Recession, as well as a loss of faith in the country's politicians."

On January 19, 2017, Obama's approval rating was 59 percent, according to Gallup.

Our country and our "leaders" are getting dumber all the time. Now they are about to release full documentation on torture. Will destroy CIA[72]

6:35 PM - 8 Dec 2014

---

72 A 2014 Senate intelligence committee report found that use of "enhanced interrogation techniques" resulted in faulty or fabricated information.

If America was under the threat of imminent attack, would Obama use torture or a kiss?

4:50 PM - 11 Dec 2014

Trump has said he supports torture even "if it doesn't work."

I just saw the movie "Unbroken" – very good except I thought the ending was weak, no retribution! And we complain about waterboarding.

10:17 PM - 2 Jan 2015

"They deserve it anyway, for what they're doing"

@WhiteGenocideTM: @realDonaldTrump Poor Jeb. I could've sworn I saw him outside Trump Tower the other day![73]

10:51 AM - 22 Jan 2016

---

73 Calls for diversity are branded "white genocide" in some white nationalist circles — and related online memes. The referring twitter account has been suspended.

Watched @davidaxelrod on @oreillyfactor and the dog hit me even after I made a big contribution to his charity. I never went bankrupt![74]

8:20 AM - 8 Oct 2014

---

74 "I used the law four times and made a tremendous thing," Trump said, defending his four bankruptcies, in a 2015 Republican debate. "I'm in business. I did a very good job."

Many journalists are honest and great – but some are knowingly dishonest and basic scum. They should. be weeded out![75]

11:42 PM - 6 Apr 2015

---

75 Trump has a long history of feeding and then baiting the media when he doesn't like the coverage he receives.

In a prescient 1999 *Doonesbury* strip, Gary Trudeau drew a cartoon Trump announcing his candidacy, which lays out his relationship with the press:

"Now, I know some of you guys choke on the fact that people love me – love me. Well, guess what? I could care less what you think. As long as I'm a candidate, you have to cover me, which is good for the Trump brand, which just gets bigger and bigger and bigger," the illustrated Trump announces, in front of a bank of microphones. "It's a win-win for me because no matter what I do, I get phenomenal, amazing, unbelievable publicity. You have to give it to me for free. You have no choice. You're sheep."

@georgewillf is perhaps the most boring political pundit on television. Got thrown off ABC like a dog. At Mar-a-Lago he was a total bust![76]

10:16 PM - 17 Apr 2015

---

76 George Will has frequently taken his shots at Trump, as he led the party to the far right of most establishment Republicans and even conservative broadcasters like Glenn Beck.

Goofy political pundit George Will spoke at Mar-a-Lago years ago. I didn't attend because he's boring & often wrong— a total dope!

10:27 AM - 19 Jun 2015

"Like all bullies, Trump is a coward," Will wrote in his column before the election, "and like all those who feel the need to boast about being strong and tough, he is neither."

How come there are no protests in favor of the two young police officers gunned down in Mississippi by two deranged animals. DEATH PENALTY![77]

5:39 AM - 11 May 2015

---

77 The killing of two Hattiesburg, Mississippi, police officers led to charges of capital murder, but the suspect died the same year, of natural causes. Nine people were charged as accessories to the murders.

"I wish we could get into the head of people who do these kind of things," Hattiesburg, Miss., Mayor Johnny DuPree told NBC, after the killings. "It was a traffic stop, and something happened to make the officer believe he needed to call for backup, which he did."

It's common rhetoric to talk about the lack of protests when police officers are murdered. But it aims to create a false equivalency between two unrelated tragedies – the shooting of unarmed African-Americans by police and the killing of police by criminals.

I just realized that if you listen to Carly Fiorina for more than ten minutes straight, you develop a massive headache. She has zero chance![78]

3:06 PM - 9 Aug 2015

---

78 Trump's use of insults to belittle women included fellow Republican U.S. presidential candidates. "Look at that face," Trump told *Rolling Stone* as he watched Fiorina speak on television. "Would anyone vote for that?"

Paul Solotaroff, in that *Rolling Stone* article, wrote, "And there, in a nutshell, is Trump's blessing and his curse: He can't seem to quit while he's ahead. The instincts that carried him out to a lead and have kept him far above the captious field are the same ones that landed him in ugly stews with ex-wives, business partners, networks, supermodels and many, many other famous women."

Dopey @BillKristol, who has lost all credibility with so many dumb statements and picks, said last week on @ Morning_Joe that Biden was in.[79]

3:19 PM - 26 Oct 2015

---

79 *Weekly Standard* Editor-in-Chief Bill Kristol (wrongly) tweeted and said on air that Joe Biden would run for president. After Trump's tweet, Kristol responded on Twitter:

The young intern who accidentally gave me that bum information apologizes. @realDonaldTrump @Morning_Joe

6:19 PM - 26 Oct 2015:

Kristol's dig was referring to a Trump retweet from the campaign trail in October 2015:

"@mygreenhippo #Benarson is now leading in the #polls in #Iowa. Too much #Monsanto in the #corn creates issues in the brain? #Trump #GOP"

Trump removed the retweet, and blamed the incident on an intern.

@DavidGregory got thrown off of TV by NBC, fired like a dog! Now he is on @CNN being nasty to me. Not nice![80]

11:10 PM - 29 Mar 2016

---

80 In Trump's tweets, people frequently are treated "like a dog" including choking (Mitt Romney in 2012), sweating (Marco Rubio), and getting fired (CNN contributor Gregory).

I hear that sleepy eyes @chucktodd will be fired like a dog from ratings starved Meet The Press? I can't imagine what is taking so long!

8:36 PM - 12 Jul 2015

Wow, great news! I hear @EWErickson of Red State was fired like a dog. If you read his tweets, you'll understand why. Just doesn't have IT!

11:57 AM - 8 Oct 2015

@GlennBeck got fired like a dog by #Fox. The Blaze is failing and he wanted to have me on his show. I said no - because he is irrelevant.

11:09 PM - 16 Dec 2015

Union Leader refuses to comment as to why they were kicked out of the ABC News debate like a dog. For starters, try getting a new publisher!

6:23 PM - 10 Jan 2016

@**BrentBozell,** one of the National Review lightweights, came to my office begging for money like a dog. Why doesn't he say that?!

8:32 PM - 22 Jan 2016

@realOllieTaylor: Isn't it time we had a president? Let goofy Glen keep Canada Cruz who can't win. The American people have Trump![81]

8:36 AM - 22 Jan 2016

---

81 Trump called Glenn Beck, who backed Sen. Ted Cruz (R-Texas), "a weird guy. He's always crying. He's a weird dude. His show is failing, by the way, so is his deal."

In the Republican primaries, Trump claimed that Cruz was ineligible to be president because he was born in Canada. Cruz is a U.S. citizen whose mother was born in Delaware.

The U.S. Constitution requires a candidate for president be a "natural born citizen."

Most legal experts agree you can be born outside of the U.S. to American parents – in part because there's no need to go through the naturalization process to become a citizen – and still be a candidate for president.

Trump also made claims linking Cruz's father to the assassination of JFK.

Boycott all Apple products until such time as Apple gives cellphone info to authorities regarding radical Islamic terrorist couple from Cal[82]

4:38 PM - 19 Feb 2016

---

82 Scott Bixby wrote in *The Guardian*, "Republican presidential candidate Donald Trump called for a boycott of Apple products until the tech giant cooperates with the FBI's demand to help unlock the iPhone of one of the San Bernardino shooters. 'What I think you ought to do is boycott Apple until such time as they give that security number,' Trump said at a town hall event in South Carolina. 'How do you like that? I just thought of that!' Trump's tweets after his call for the Apple boycott were all sent from an Apple iPhone."

I wonder if @megynkelly and her flunkies have written their scripts yet about my debate performance tonight. No matter how well I do - bad![83]

4:38 PM - 19 Feb 2016

---

83 During the first GOP debate, Megyn Kelly said, "You've called women you don't like fat pigs, dogs, slobs, and disgusting animals." Then: "Your Twitter account has several disparaging comments about women's looks. You once told a contestant on 'Celebrity Apprentice' it would be a pretty picture to see her on her knees. Does that sound to you like the temperament of a man we should elect as president, and how will you answer the charge from Hillary Clinton, who was likely to be the Democratic nominee, that you are part of the war on women?"

Trump's response:

"I think the big problem this country has is being politically correct. I've been challenged by so many people and I don't, frankly, have time for total political correctness. And to be honest with you, this country doesn't have time, either."

Re Megyn Kelly quote: "you could see there was blood coming out of her eyes, blood coming out of her wherever" (NOSE). Just got on w/thought

8:46 AM - 8 Aug 2015

If crazy @megynkelly didn't cover me so much on her terrible show, her ratings would totally tank. She is so average in so many ways!

8:16 AM - 19 Mar 2016

I have a judge in the Trump University civil case, Gonzalo Curiel (San Diego), who is very unfair. An Obama pick. Totally biased- hates Trump![84]

5:45 PM - 30 May 2016

---

84 Trump called Indiana-born federal Judge Gonzalo P. Curiel a "Mexican," implying he couldn't be impartial because "we are building a wall between here and Mexico ... I think that's why he's doing it."

Goofy Elizabeth Warren, sometimes referred to as Pocahontas, pretended to be a Native American in order to advance her career. Very racist![85]

7:28 PM - 11 Jun 2016

---

85 Trump has a history of using slurs in reference to Native Americans. In 1993, testifying at a House subcommittee about the Mashantucket Pequots, who run the Foxwoods Resort Casino in Connecticut, he said: "They don't look like Indians to me. And they don't look like Indians to Indians."

According to *The Washington Post*, Trump testified that, "organized crime is rmapant in Indian casinos around the nations...At the time, the developer was fighing the expansion of gambling on tribal lands, a direct threat to his casino empire."

The Post also reported that Trump secretly funded an ad campaign in 2000 suggesting a proposed casino for the St. Regis Mohawk nation would draw "criminals and drug users."

U.S. Sen. Warren (D-Mass.) tweeted that Trump and Pence were "Two small, insecure, weak men who use hate & fear to divide our country & our people."

Elizabeth Warren, often referred to as Pocahontas, just misrepresented me and spoke glowingly about Crooked Hillary, who she always hated!

11:12 PM - 25 Jul 2016

No one has worse judgement than Hillary Clinton - corruption and devastation follows her wherever she goes[86]

11:59 PM - 28 Jul 2016

---

[86] After Clinton accepted the Democratic Party nomination, Trump fired off a series of tweets that appeared to be a reaction to Clinton's: "Imagine him in the Oval Office facing a real crisis. A man you can bait with a tweet is not a man we can trust with nuclear weapons."

Trump told Fox News' Chris Wallace in December 2016 that he didn't need daily briefings: "I don't have to be told the same thing in the same words every single day for the next eight years."

Classified documents reviewed by *Mother Jones*, sent to intelligence analysts, suggested keeping information on security threats short and free of nuance.

In January 2016, Trump told Axios: "I like bullets or I like as little as possible. I don't need, you know, 200-page reports on something that can be handled on a page. That I can tell you."

Hillary Clinton should not be given national security briefings in that she is a lose cannon with extraordinarily bad judgement & insticts.

8:57 PM - 29 Jul 2016
• Denver, CO

Reuters reported in May 2017 that Trump "likes single-page memos and visual aids like maps, charts, graphs and photos. National Security Council officials have strategically included Trump's name in 'as many paragraphs as we can because he keeps reading if he's mentioned.'"

Also in May, *The Washington Post* reported "President Trump revealed highly classified information to the Russian foreign minister and ambassador in a White House meeting last week, according to current and former U.S. officials, who said that Trump's disclosures jeopardized a critical source of intelligence on the Islamic State."

Current and former U.S. officials told *The Post* "Trump's decision to do so risks cooperation from an ally that has access to the inner workings of the Islamic State. After Trump's meeting, senior White House officials took steps to contain the damage, placing calls to the CIA and National Security Agency."

I was viciously attacked by Mr. Khan at the Democratic Convention. Am I not allowed to respond? Hillary voted for the Iraq war, not me!![87]

9:32 AM - 31 Jul 2016

---

[87] At the Democratic National Convention, Muslim-American Gold Star parent Khizr Khan, standing with his wife, Ghazala, spoke of his son, Army Capt. Humayun Khan, who was killed in action in Iraq and posthumously awarded the Purple Heart and Bronze Star. Khizr Khan asked whether Trump had ever read the Constitution.

Trump fired back in a series of tweets, including one questioning why Ghazala Khan hadn't spoken. Later she wrote in *The Washington Post*: "Donald Trump said I had nothing to say. I do. My son Humayun Khan, an Army captain, died 12 years ago in Iraq. He loved America."

Some day, when things calm down, I'll tell the real story of @JoeNBC and his very insecure long-time girlfriend, @morningmika. Two clowns![88]

9 AM - 22 Aug 2016

---

88 Some media critics suggested *Morning Joe* hosts Joe Scarborough and Mika Brzezinski had a too-close relationship with Trump as he campaigned. But after raising questions about Trump's mental stability as well as his worrisome suggestions that he might use nuclear weapons (Brzezinski), the then-candidate went on the attack.

In *The Washington Post* Callum Borchers wrote: "When Trump claimed not to 'know anything about David Duke' in an interview on CNN in late February, declining to disavow the former Ku Klux Klan leader's support, Scarborough called the candidate's remark 'disqualifying.'"

I don't watch or do @Morning_Joe anymore. Small audience, low ratings! I hear Mika has gone wild with hate. Joe is Joe. They lost their way!

11:12 PM - 25 Jul 2016

Wacky @NYTimes-Dowd, who hardly knows me, makes up things that I never said for her boring interviews and column. A neurotic dope![89]

11:12 PM - 25 Jul 2016

89 From a *New York Times* transcript of an interview with Trump: "If you see something or get something where you feel that I'm wrong, and you have some info – I would love to hear it," he told *The New York Times*. "You can call me, Arthur can call me, I would love to hear. The only one who can't call me is Maureen [Dowd, opinion columnist]. She treats me too rough."

Voter fraud! Crooked Hillary Clinton even got the questions to a debate, and nobody says a word. Can you imagine if I got the questions?[90]

11:24 AM - 17 Oct 2016

90 Wikileaks published an email from Democratic strategist Donna Brazile, who was at the time a commentator for CNN, saying: "From time to time, I get the questions in advance." Brazile said she was referring to prep work for a panel. She denied providing an advanced town hall question to Clinton, however a related question was asked the next day in a town hall with the Democratic candidate. "To be perfectly clear, we have never, ever given a town hall question to anyone beforehand," a CNN spokeswoman told *Politico*.

WikiLeaks reveals Clinton camp's work with 'VERY friendly and malleable reporters' #Drain-TheSwamp #CrookedHillary[91]

6:46 PM - 21 Oct 2016

---

91 A U.S. intelligence report identified Russian officials, directed by Vladamir Putin, who provided DNC-hacked materials to Wikileaks, according to a January 5, 2017, *Reuters* article.

"You sure have to hand it to the Russians," wrote Jim Rutenberg in *The New York Times*. "They understand the power of free-flowing information, how it can upend government and politics. It's why they don't let information flow too freely in their own country. And it's why, if United States intelligence assessments are correct, they have worked so hard to send it roaring through ours."

I worked hard with Bill Ford to keep the Lincoln plant in Kentucky. I owed it to the great State of Kentucky for their confidence in me![92]

9:15 PM - 17 Nov 2016

92 Ford wasn't leaving Kentucky in the first place: *The Washington Post* confirmed that Ford had been planning to relocate production of its Lincoln MKC model to Mexico from Kentucky, but had never planned on moving the factory.

I settled the Trump University lawsuit for a small fraction of the potential award because as President I have to focus on our country.[93]

8:34 AM - 19 Nov 2016

---

93 Trump settled for $25 million; the fraud was for around $40 million (5,000 students), so his "small fraction" was just over 60 percent of the amount.

The Theater must always be a safe and special place.The cast of Hamilton was very rude last night to a very good man, Mike Pence. Apologize![94]

8:34 AM - 19 Nov 2016

94 During a visit to the show, *Hamilton* star Brandon Victor Dixon addressed then-Vice President Elect Mike Pence saying the cast was worried "your new administration will not protect us, our planet, our children, our parents, or defend us and uphold our inalienable rights."

In *The Guardian*, Arwa Mahdawi wrote, "Conservatives are impressively adept at belittling politically correct [easily offended] snowflakes one minute and flying into fits of ideological outrage the next. Snowflakes are to be mocked because they take things personally; their feelings are hurt. The outrage of populist correctness, however, is framed more as righteous indignation. It is not you who is offended. You are offended on behalf of the people. On behalf of your country. Your outrage is morally superior."

The cast and producers of Hamilton, which I hear is highly overrated, should immediately apologize to Mike Pence for their terrible behavior[95]

6:22 AM - 20 Nov 2016

---

95 This tweet came in the same news cycle where it was announced Trump would pay a $25 million settlement in a fraud case over Trump University.

Trump's former senior adviser, Steve Bannon, says Trump is adept at creating distractions and calls him "master of the head fake."

I watched parts of @nbcsnl Saturday Night Live last night. It is a totally one-sided, biased show - nothing funny at all. Equal time for us?[96]

8:26 AM - 20 Nov 2016

96 "Alec Baldwin deserves a Presidential Medal of Freedom," former Late Night Show host David Letterman said in an interview with *New York* magazine in March, 2017. "Sadly, he's not going to get it from this president."

In a CNN op-ed, Dean Obeidallah commented on Trump's call for cancelling *SNL*: "Think about that for a moment – the GOP presidential nominee was calling for a comedy show to be canceled because he didn't like the way it was mocking him. No wonder Trump admires autocratic leaders like Egypt's Abdel Fattah el-Sisi, who effectively banned Egypt's version of *The Daily Show* because he didn't like the way it portrayed him. Bassem Youseff, the show's star comedian, was subsequently forced to flee Cairo and go into exile."

Prior to the election it was well known that I have interests in properties all over the world. Only the crooked media makes this a big deal![97]

9:14 PM - 21 Nov 2016

---

97 In his thoughtful *New Yorker* essay "Why Trump's Conflicts of Interest Won't Hurt Him," James Surowiecki made the case that Trump, like former Ohio congressman James Traficant before him, uses his D.C.-outsider image to trample on traditional social mores. Traficant was convicted of bribery, racketeering and tax evasion yet served from 1985-2002, until Congress forcibly evicted him.

Voters of all stripes tend to look the other way when their interests appear to be represented. "In fact," Surowiecki wrote, "seventy-three per cent of Republicans told a *Politico/Morning Consult* survey that Trump's business interests would help him do a better job."

Such a beautiful and important evening! The forgotten man and woman will never be forgotten again. We will all come together as never before [98]

Nov 9, 2016 06:36:58 AM

---

98 On November 8, 2016, Donald John Trump was elected the 45th president of the United States.

Since then, his approval rating has hovered around 39 percent, about the same as President Gerald Ford's after he pardoned Richard Nixon.

Through executive orders and memos, Trump has cracked down on illegal immigration, withdrawn from the Paris Climate agreement and the Trans-Pacific Partnership (TPP) and approved the Keystone XL and Dakota Access pipelines. He's continued to push a ban on people from seven predominantly Muslim countries, despite court orders that deemed them unconstitutional. In its ruling, the 9th Circuit Court of Appeals even referred to a Trump tweet:

Jun 5, 2017 08:20:17 PM That's right, we need a TRAVEL BAN for certain DANGEROUS countries, not some politically correct term that won't help us protect our people!

The court ruled the order "exceeded the scope of the authority delegated to him by Congress."

In her concession speech on November 9, 2016, Hillary Clinton told supporters: "Donald Trump is going to be our president. We owe him an open mind and a chance to lead. Our constitutional democracy demands our participation, not just every four years but all the time. So let's do all we can to keep advancing the causes and values we all hold dear."

Epilogue

The tweets come fast, and one seems to overwrite the last. It's hard to keep up, with all the losers and dopes, the fools, the fake news, the conspiracies, all the winning and the threats.

So, when can we look away? How do we take a moment to reflect on a single moment, before the next tweetstorm blows in?

It seems appropriate to pause on an event that – while tragic – feels as likely as any other to get lost in the scrolling feed.

On a fall Saturday in central Virginia, Heather Heyer walked through Charlottesville's downtown mall along with her friends who were protesting a demonstration of far-right nationalists.

Am in Bedminster for meetings & press conference on V.A. & all that we have done, and are doing, to make it better-but Charlottesville sad!

1:00 PM - 12 Aug 2017

At 1:42 p.m., a white supremacist drove his car into the crowd, running over Heyer, killing her, and wounding 19 others.

Two Virginia state troopers also died as they monitored the protest. The Bell 407 helicopter piloted by H. Jay Cullen, 48, and Berke Bates, who would have turned 41 the next day, crashed in the woods in Albemarle County.

We ALL mustbe united & condemn all that hate stands for. There is no place for this kind of violence in America. Lets come together as one!

1:19 PM - Aug 12, 2017

At 3:34 Trump made a statement during a bill signing at his golf course in Bedminster, New Jersey:

"We condemn in the strongest possible terms this egregious display of hatred, bigotry and violence on many sides. On many sides. It's been going on for a long time in our country. Not Donald Trump, not Barack Obama, this has been going on for a long, long time."

He then said:

"Our country is doing very well in so many ways, we have absolute record employment. We have on employment the lowest it has been in almost 17 years. We have companies pouring into our country. Car companies and so many others, they're coming back to our country. We are renegotiating trade deals to make them great for country and great for the American worker. We have so many incredible things happening in our country."

That evening, Trump tweeted:

Condolences to the family of the young woman killed today, and best regards to all of those injured, in Charlottesville, Virginia. So sad!

Aug 12, 2017 06:25:25 PM

Later that day the White House issued a clarification of the president's statement, which didn't seem to stray far from the original comments about violence, on many sides. Then another clarification appeared later that day, this one explicitly criticizing hate groups.

Made additional remarks on Charlottesville and realize once again that the #Fake News Media will never be satisfied...truly bad people!

5:29 PM - 14 Aug 2017

The day after this tweet, at a press conference at Trump Tower, the president seemed again to suggest fault was shared between far-right extremists in Charlottesville, some of whom carried Nazi flags, and the protesters who demonstrated against them, including Heyer, who was run down by a car:

"There is blame on both sides. I have no doubt about it – and you don't have any doubt about it either," Trump said. "You also had people that were very fine people on both sides."

The public is learning (even more so) how dishonest the Fake News is. They totally misrepresent what I say about hate, bigotry etc. Shame!

Sad to see the history and culture of our great country being ripped apart with the removal of our beautiful statues and monuments. You.....

...can't change history, but you can learn from it. Robert E Lee, Stonewall Jackson - who's next, Washington, Jefferson? So foolish! Also...

..the beauty that is being taken out of our cities, towns and parks will be greatly missed and never able to be comparably replaced!

17 Aug 2017

On Aug. 22, a little over a week after Heyer was murdered, Trump flew to Phoenix to hold a rally. At one point in his remarks, he spoke for about 30 minutes in an attempt to clarify his reaction to the violence in Charlottesville.

"Trump took a disastrous and losing talking point and repeated it over and over again when absolutely no one wanted or needed him to do that," wrote Ed Kilgore, in *New York* magazine. "He actually made it all worse by once again arguing that taking down Confederate monuments is the same as attacking George Washington."

Phoenix crowd last night was amazing - a packed house. I love the Great State of Arizona. Not a fan of Jeff Flake, weak on crime & border!

9:20 AM - Aug 23, 2017

Last night in Phoenix I read the things from my statements on Charlottesville that the Fake News Media didn't cover fairly. People got it!

9:40 AM - Aug 23, 2017

In an appearance on MTV, the Rev. Robert Lee IV – the fourth great-nephew of Civil war Gen. Robert E. Lee – joined Heyer's mother, Susan Bro. Lee had this to say:

"We have made my ancestor an idol of white supremacy, racism and hate. As a pastor, it is my moral duty to speak out against racism, America's original sin. Today, I call on all of us, with privilege and power to answer God's call to confront racism and white supremacy head-on. We can find inspiration in the Black Lives Matter movement; the women who marched in the women's march in January; and especially Heather Heyer, who died fighting for her beliefs in Charlottesville."

"I always encouraged her to be strong and strong-minded," Bro told NBC in an interview, "even though that wasn't always easy to raise. But I was always proud of what she was doing."

Heyer's father, Mark, told the *New York Daily News*: "She was to the point. She told people like she thought. She didn't mince words with them."

Her grandfather, Elwood Shrader, said this at her service: "She realized we all need forgiveness and we all must extend forgiveness. As we think about her today, we're very proud of her."

Memorial service today for beautiful and incredible Heather Heyer, a truly special young woman. She will be long remembered by all!

7:58 AM - Aug 16, 2017

At Heyer's memorial an overflow crowd gathered inside a theater in downtown Charlottesville.

"My child's famous Facebook post was, 'If you're not outraged, you're not paying attention," Bro said. "She paid attention. She made a lot of us pay attention."